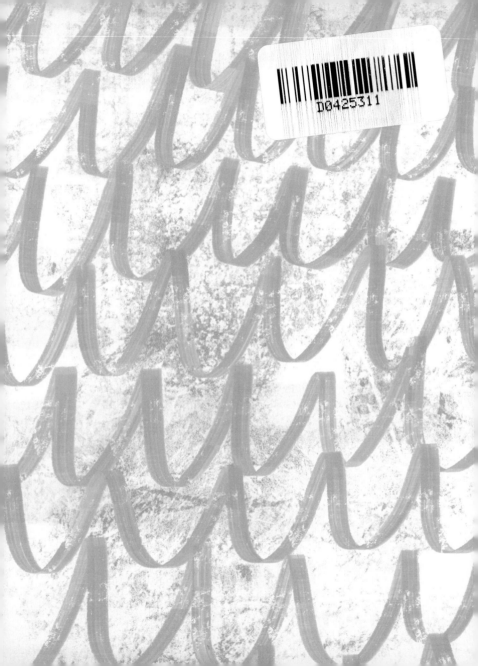

The Little Book of
LAGER

Melanie,

Finally, I wrote one you'll like!

Thank you for always being the bestest big sister anyone could ask for. You are so loving and strong. I am more proud of you than you could ever know, and I am looking forward to us growing old disgracefully together.

Love you to the moon and back.

Titch x

Mum and Dad,

You are my inspirations and my bedrocks. Thank you for everything you do, and have done; you're incredible. X

The Little Book of

LAGER

A guide to the world's most
popular style of beer

Melissa Cole

Hardie Grant

BOOKS

CONTENTS

INTRODUCTION

I love a good lager. In fact, if you give me enough sunshine and a holiday I'm more than happy to drink pretty much any lager you put in my hand, because the last thing I want to do is think about my work when I have a few days off. Yes, it's likely to be what the purists would tell you is a 'crappy' lager, but, do you know what? I work hard and I deserve it, and so do you.

So, with this in mind, I'm not here to tell you what to drink, I'm just here to provide you with information on how you might be able to drink broader and better... that's it.

Hence why I've chosen to write my fourth book about lager. It is a love letter to the world's favourite style of beer. In fact, it's the world's favourite alcoholic beverage, and potentially the most misunderstood, despite that fact; and whilst you could argue that a lot of what calls itself lager technically isn't (more on that later), what you can't argue about is its incredible popularity.

Another great thing about lager is that a lot of brands have the most brilliant stories behind them; as a journalist by training, these are the kinds of things that get me out of bed in the morning (albeit sometimes a little slowly!).

So, whether you want an ice-cold, own-brand supermarket sipper or a more esoteric Oktoberfest offering in your hand, there's absolutely no arguing that not only do lagers help make the world rub along a little more easily on a social level, it's also a fascinating and multi-faceted style that owes its name to a process of brewing that changed the face of the beer world forever.

WHAT IS LAGER?

What do you think of when I say lager? I imagine it's a pale yellow, fizzy, icy liquid that doesn't merit much attention. It's more a means to an end than a gastronomic ride.

But what if I told you that lagers can be strong or weak, as light in colour as pale winter sun or midnight black, as fey as a fairy's kiss or as texturally rich as a dessert wine?

There are also impersonators that look and feel like a lager but are deemed to be hybrids. There are lagers that have lashings of aromatic hops and seem to have more in common with pale ales than the relatively commercial offerings out there; and there are methods of making these that differ from a standard lager, but they drink as deliciously as their 'true' counterparts.

All of these things are wrapped up in these pages, with simple explanations and some more information on what I consider to be some of the world's best examples.

NO, SERIOUSLY, WHAT IS LAGER?

We get the word 'lager' from the German *'lagern'*, which means 'to store'. So, in reality, lager is actually a process more than it is a style, as lots of different styles of beers are lagered. Baltic porters are just one example, and that dark, strong beer is almost as far away from what people think of as 'lager' as you can get.

So how is it made?

GRAIN OF TRUTH

The foundation on which every beer stands is a malt base, but what is malt exactly? To put it very simply, it's a grain — normally barley — that's been fooled into thinking it's springtime to start germination, and then stopped in its tracks by a careful drying and toasting process.

The level to which you toast the grains in the malting process gives you not only varying levels of accessible starches and active enzymes in the grains — the latter of which will convert the starches into sugars for the yeast to munch on and produce alcohol and CO_2 — but also accounts for the colour and flavour in your beer.

The flavours (and colours) from malts can range from the lightest white bread, through to wholemeal, caramel and toffee, to raisin and milk chocolate to dark chocolate, through to the deepest espresso. These can then be mixed with a host of other malted and unmalted grains, like wheat, oats, sorghum, rye and others, to allow for as simple or as complex a flavour profile as the brewer desires.

The very best malting barley is considered to come from maritime climates, and the UK is said by most brewers to have the best in the world (although, of course, that may also be a little bit of the good kind of national pride talking!).

WONDERFUL WATER

Water, water everywhere – but not for making beer... well, OK, that's not strictly true, but if you want to lay a bit of beer knowledge on people, then you can tell them that in the brewhouse the water used for brewing is called 'liquor' and 'water' is used for washing things. I know, it's all a bit unnecessarily complicated, but that's brewers for you!

One of the reasons for differentiating is that brewers regularly treat the water they get, often from the mains, with what are known as 'brewer's salts'. This is the process of treating the water with different minerals to mimic the natural water source of classic beer styles.

So, for example, one of the reasons that Burton-on-Trent became renowned for its IPAs is that its natural water source is very rich in gypsum, or calcium sulphate, as it's scientifically known, which creates a more pronounced dry, clean bitterness.

Whereas London, historically renowned for its porters, is known to have a calcium carbonate-rich water supply, more suited to malt-forward beers and creating a rounder mouthfeel.

HOP ON BOARD

A hop is a climbing plant and its use in, and cultivation for, modern brewing now means that hops are used in nearly all but the tiniest percentage of the world's beer.

Hops, like grapes, develop a terroir. In case you were frightened to ask anyone what terroir means (I was when a very fancy wine writer said it for the first time to me), it's the effect that the hours of sunlight, the soil and the general climate has on a crop. In this case, I'm talking about hops, but you'll more generally hear it spoken of in terms of grapes.

Regardless of their original species, within a decade or so of having been planted in a different country, hops will develop characteristics that have migrated so far away from their forebears that they are often renamed. For example, NZ Cascade has now been renamed Taiheke, but it originated from the US Cascade hop that, in turn, first came from a cross between a UK hop and a European hop.

Every step of the way is important in the development of that hop's characteristics, but the defining factor in what it smells and tastes like today is the terroir that it has been shaped by most recently. Anyway, my point is that hops have followed a similar path to that of 'old' and 'new world' wines a few decades ago, which brings us neatly back to that word 'terroir'.

Traditionally the UK has been known for its subtly bitter hops, with restrained aroma characteristics like tobacco, hedgerow fruit and mown grass. A lot of Central and Eastern European hops have similar characteristics to UK hops, but many of them have also been developed specifically for delicate styles like Pilsners and other lagers or ales, so you get more subtle and restrained notes like woody herbs, black pepper and fresh hay.

The USA is known for its more aggressively bitter hops, with big citrus, pine, rose and marijuana aromas and flavours. Australian hops tend towards the US versions with some fairly hefty bitterness, but with more subtle apricot, peach and lemony flavours and aromas and the odd foray into more floral lands.

Then there are New Zealand hops, which have some of the most interesting and complex aromas and flavours being developed anywhere (in my opinion). Their bitterness can be subtle to booming and aromas and flavours range from Sauvignon Blanc to lime zest, cherry blossom and beyond.

As the spread of beer pioneers continues globally and, to a certain extent, the climate emergency deepens, other areas of the world have also been able to start growing hops too. Spain now has a thriving hop business, Japan is well known for some very unusual varieties and South Africa is another hub of hop development, so check the back of your bottles or cans to get some good clues!

YEAST IS THE BEAST

Yeast, that beautiful single-celled fungi that takes in sugars and expels alcohol and CO_2 is the most critical ingredient in beer and was considered a magical element before science identified its presence.

Ancient civilisations believed that deities gifted the alcoholic element of their brews, the most famous evidence for which is the Hymn to Ninkasi, the Sumerian goddess of beer. The praise for this goddess was immortalised in a stone tablet in 1800 BC and also doubles up as a recipe for beer. And even the infamous *Reinheitsgebot*, the German purity law, didn't recognise yeast as one of the core ingredients of beer when the first draft was written in Bavaria in the early 1500s. But now, thanks to technology, we understand more about yeast than we ever have before (there'll be more on the *Reinheitsgebot* later!).

Yeasts are now so diverse that it's difficult to explain things simply, so I'm just going to stick to the most important type of the *Saccharomyces* family to making lager.

The strain of yeast most commonly used for lagers is *Saccharomyces pastorianus* (named for Louis Pasteur who identified it as the most efficient yeast to make cold maturation beers). These diligent yeasts like to ferment at cool temperatures over a week or so and then, quite literally, chill out for a few weeks; by which I mean stay in cold storage. So now you should be a bit clearer on why I say it's a process rather than a style, but has come to be generically known as lager over the years.

ENJOY MORE

OK, that's not an edict to go and drink more, I just wanted to ask you to stop and smell the beer (and the roses if there happen to be any nearby!). The reason I say this is that all too often we don't take the time to appraise our beers before guzzling them down.

Now, I'm not saying that you not smelling your beer is necessarily a bad thing. Just finished mowing the lawn in the hot sun? Grabbing a frosty one and finishing the first third in one gulp is a thing of great beauty. Just finished a hard sports game or a run? Heck, grab that cold beer and reward yourself (in fact, science says you're doing a good thing, as beer is proven to have better recovery properties than water), but if you want to really get to know, and understand, what it is you're drinking, then you have to get your nose involved.

Why do I say that? Well, it's because the nose knows. It's your very first line of defence against nasty tastes and poorly made or kept products. It's a result of evolution, it's what tells us whether something is good or bad and, most likely, whether we'll like it or not.

As someone who judges beers the world over, I can frequently discard 30–50% of rounds of beer on smell alone. I can tell that there's something wrong and why just from the smell of it (not that I'm suggesting you will be able to... just yet!) and if you stop and smell your beer, using cautious little bunny sniffs first before inhaling deeply, then you'll really get to grips with what it is that you are about to try.

The other reason I advocate stopping to smell your beer is this: if you are having the very best night out with friends, a romantic evening with a loved one, or just a peaceful, contemplative moment with yourself, then if you stop and smell the beer, the next time you drink it, or perhaps even years from now, you may be gifted with the memory of how you felt in that moment. Smell is the most evocative of memory nudges and that, my friends, is worth its weight in lager.

The Kölsch and Altbier Glass
This glass is a small, straight-sided delicate glass, because these beers are very delicate and best drunk in small, appreciative quantities if you'd like to get the best from them.

The Pilsner Glass
Classically, the Pilsner glass is a short-stemmed, lightly-angled glass, designed to hold a larger pour, which better suits the more robust nature of the beer style.

TEMPERATURE AND GLASSWARE

Let's tackle temperature first as it's probably one of the most asked questions that I get in beer tastings. There's a fairly useful rule of thumb, and that's to drink it however the heck you like it because you have worked hard for the money to pay for it. Seriously, I'm not the beer police, you do you.

However, if you want to get the very best out of your beers then I do have some fairly loose advice on how to approach it.

Firstly, beers designed to be drunk fresh, like Pilsners, Helles, Kölsch, IPLs and Viennas, are all best served cold in my opinion. You can go as high as 6°C (43°F) for something like a Vienna, but I'd say the rest are best served between 2–4°C (36–39°F).

However, for the more complex, aged beers, the ones with a bit more heft, alcoholic strength, complex aromas and flavours, I do recommend that you serve these a little warmer, about 8–10°C (46–50°F).

And, just as I won't be prescriptive about what temperature you drink your beer at, I'm not going to get overly sniffy about what glass you drink it from either (or even if you drink it from a can or bottle, but it does get a little more difficult to do the smelling part!). However, there are a few classic glass shapes that have developed over the years to go with specific styles.

The Bock Glass
This bigger, beefier beer benefits from a wider mouth, to better appreciate the aromas and is therefore a bit more chalice-like in its appearance.

KEEP IT CLEAN

There is just one thing I'll say about glassware, and it's that I see too many social media posts with what can only be described as horrifyingly filthy glasses. However, just to show that no one is infallible, I'll never forget noticing that one of the glasses was a bit dirty on the cover of my first book *Let Me Tell You About Beer* two minutes after being utterly euphoric that I had my advance copy, then gently banging my head on my desk for a further two minutes after I realised. Anyway... this is a case of do as I say, not as I do!

There are obvious clues for a dirty glass – smudged fingerprints, remnants of lipstick on the rim – but the dead giveaway that it's not clean enough is that the bubbles will adhere to the inside of the glass. If your glass is perfectly clean, you should be able to see straight into the liquid.

The best way to wash beer glasses is to get some very hot soapy water, scrub them thoroughly inside, then rinse in very hot water, ensuring the water is cascading evenly off the inside and not sticking anywhere. After that, leave to air dry (dish towels are rarely perfectly clean and are likely to leave fibres on the inside).

Right, those are just some basics, but I bet you're really thirsty by now – I know I am – so let's get to the good part: the beers!

Chapter One

Gold

I know, a bit vague, but let's be honest, a lot of us drink with our eyes and 'gold' or 'blonde' is now as much a colour designation as 'light' has become a descriptor of lower carb or calorie food or drink.

Here, you may be pleased to know, it is distinctly more about the former, and you'll find Helles, Kellerbiers, Zwickelbiers, Dortmunders and other, more familiar names, like Pilsner.

What this will demonstrate is that, even if you've been drinking the same brand of 'lager' forever and a day, there is a whole host of variation at the lighter end of the spectrum you may never have even thought of trying and this will hopefully give you the confidence to order outside of 'the usual'.

HELLES

There is very little doubt that there is no other beer style in the world that displays the subtlety, the approachability, the balance or the elegance that a Helles does.

Playing off the German word for 'light', Helles is one of the most approachable styles of lager you can possibly enjoy. Introduced by Gabriel Sedlmayr II in 1894, it has remained the everyday beer of the Bavarian region ever since.

As much a product of the incredibly soft water in the region as it is of the glorious traditional German hops, it is a world-class lesson in balance and drinkability.

GERMAN PILSNER

When you drink any commercial beer that says Pilsner, it's rarely referencing what many think of as the 'original' Pilsner. Instead, it's actually comparing itself to the more aggressive German version, which is a very different beast.

Whereas, the Czech versions are renowned for their rather obvious hint of diacetyl (a fermentation by-product that creates a slightly slick mouthfeel and, in higher concentrations, a cinema-popcorn buttery toffee aroma and flavour), these are abrasive, briskly carbonated and brightly hopped.

The hops are a key component to these beers, because they bring a brazen hop character that is also, somehow, a study in restraint – possibly due to their terroir. The Tettnanger, Mittelfrüh, Hallertauer and Spalt hops give this peppery, herbal belt without whacking you round the chops like New World hops have a tendency to do.

When in Germany, it's more common to ask for a Pils than it is to call it by its full name, and a frothing glass of this, in even the cheesiest of *biergartens*, is a thing of beauty and wonder.

DORTMUNDER

A style that is a little difficult to define as it has waxed and waned in definition over the years but the easiest way to describe it is as a strong Helles-style beer. The level of alcohol can be up to 6%, so it can seem a little sweet if not served at properly cold temperatures. It can come off as a little cloying so I would suggest no more than an initial 4°C (39°F) – make sure you get that right!

MAIBOCK

Maibock was brewed, as the name suggests, by May, and as a strong beer to be tucked away during the warmer months, because brewing laws dictated that beer couldn't be made in that time due the temperature variations, a sensible strategy as it would have been pre-refrigeration and cooling technology.

It was first brewed in the central town of Einbeck, Germany. The dialectic pronunciation is *'ein Bock'*, meaning 'billy goat' in German, which is why you'll often see the labels depicted with a male goat on it, complete with a hairy chin!

ZWICKEL/KELLERBIER

These are beers that come direct from tanks in cellars. They can be fairly faithfully recreated in package by ensuring the beer is unfiltered and unpasteurised and made with that all-important soft water profile, which gives them that wonderful fresh bread character that is their main moreish defining characteristic.

CZECH PILSNER

Allegedly born in the town of Pilsen — an argument for more dedicated beer historians than myself — there's no doubt that the city's Pilsner Urquell is still considered the gold standard for the Czech Pilsner style.

Using the decoction method (see page 35 for details), it produces a deeper, richer — almost bordering on copper — colour and, as mentioned in German Pils, it also has a distinct toffee caramel to it.

The other thing that differentiates the Czech-style Pilsner is its use of the altogether softer Saaz hops, which are grown in abundance in the country to satisfy demand.

Augustiner
Lagerbier
Hell

ABV	5.2%
COUNTRY OF ORIGIN	Germany
GREAT WITH	*Weisswurst*
	(Bavarian sausage)
ALSO TRY	Camden Hells
	4.6%, UK

I simply cannot leave my favourite German Helles beer out of this section; it's physically impossible. It is a thing of such simple joy that it is almost tactile... mind you, they should be good at making this beer by now, having been founded in 1328.

The brewery itself is almost a pilgrimage; apt given that it was originally founded by monks prior to the secularisation of Germany. It not only has its own bore water that reaches over 200 m (0.2 km) deep, it also has its own floor maltings (where the grain is prepared for the brewing process), a rarity in today's world.

The Hell is the colour of an early primrose, with an immediate aroma of fresh-cut grass and an incredibly brisk carbonation, but it's the incredible flavour and finish that makes this such an enduring classic. I can't put it better than my good friend and fellow beer writer, Matt Curtis: 'When you taste it, there's an initial note of freshly baked white bread, which is soon snapped away by a rasping, herbal bitterness.'

The Helles style of lager caused quite a stir with the Bavarian old guard of brewing when it was first introduced by Spaten in 1894. They thought it was taking too much influence from the Bohemia-based upstart Josef Groll in Pilzen, and that beer should be brown. Given the way that a lot of traditional beer drinkers in the UK have responded to the introduction of 'craft' beers, you have to say that history is, indeed, repetitive!

Drygate
Bearface
Lager

ABV	4.4%
COUNTRY OF ORIGIN	Scotland
GREAT WITH	Scotch pie
ALSO TRY	Tröegs Sunshine Pils 4.5%, USA

You have to love a good old-fashioned bit of Scottish cheekiness and this embodies it in beer format. Drygate brewpub sits slap bang on the doorstep of the rather enormous Tennent's Brewery in Glasgow, which produces Scotland's favourite lager. It is a partnership between this behemoth brand and long-established craft brewery Williams Brothers.

The name 'Bearface lager' comes from the fact that it was the first beer to be produced on the site. Someone mentioned that it was 'pure barefaced cheek' to produce a lager when perched on the edge of the Tennent's Brewery – and the name just stuck.

Made with hefty doses of American hops, it is a clean, easy-drinking citrus, herbal number with a refreshing but not aggressive carbonation that roars across your palate, making you quickly ready for another sip, and another, and before you know it, it's all gone.

Wellpark Brewery, where Scotland's favourite lager brand Tennent's is made, was actually originally known as the Drygate Brewery when it was founded in 1556. It changed its name in 1740, which makes it Glasgow's longest continuous recorded commercial enterprise. You can also visit the last tiny part of the well that it's named after, which is visible round the back of the brewery, although you may have to ask for directions!

Notch
Brewing
Zwickel

ABV	4.5%
COUNTRY OF ORIGIN	USA
GREAT WITH	Popcorn chicken
ALSO TRY	Veltins Grevensteiner
	5.2%, Germany

Notch Brewing is one of those breweries that will always get nerdy lager lovers excited. They founded their brewery on a love of sessionable beers and that has led them to brew styles from all over the world, but it's those fantastic lagers that really get people talking.

My personal favourite is the Zwickel, brewed using the decoction method (see box) that produces a richer malt character, which means it carries the liberal application of Spalt and Sterling hops very well.

The appearance is a vibrant sunset gold, with a really tight white head on it. There is an aroma of mandarin, heather and pepper, all laid out on a lightly bready malt body – lager perfection in my book.

Decoction is a method that creates a more complex flavour profile from simple malt bills (the mix of grains that make up the beer). Generally, about a third of the mash is removed and heated to a higher temperature in a special vessel before being returned to the mix. This gives it a complexity of flavour and better yield of fermentable sugars. Some would argue it's unnecessary with today's exceptional malting technologies and others say it gives a unique characteristic.

Zwickel is often cited as being a lower alcohol version of a German *kellerbier* (see page 25), but this is disputed by some beer historians. What is absolutely indisputable is the flavoursome joy of unfiltered and unpasteurised lagers. Both filtration and pasteurisation strip the flavours out of any beer; it's why most commercial versions tend to have a similar profile and lack excitement. My first experience of an unfiltered lager was in the cellars of Budweiser Budvar in the Czech Republic, and it's entirely possible there are still nail marks in the cellar doorframe where they had to drag me out, kicking and screaming.*

*(OK, not really. But it felt like it!)

Muflon
11°

ABV	4.5%
COUNTRY OF ORIGIN	Czech Republic
GREAT WITH	Young goat's cheese
ALSO TRY	Holba 11°
	4.7%, Czech Republic

The Czech Republic has been undergoing something of a brewing renaissance in the last 10 years or so and Muflon was one of the breweries that kicked that off.

Originally a brewing equipment company, it's no huge surprise that they have the chops to create great beer (although I have experienced instances where the two don't go hand-in-hand that well, that is fortunately not the case here!) and have been winning awards pretty much since they started.

The 11° is a great showcase for Premiant hops, which are like traditional Saaz that, if you have ever drunk any of the traditional Czech Pilsners, you'll instinctively know the smell of, but here it is definitely dialled up to maximum.

A lovely lime blossom aroma, with a dried hay and wholemeal bread body, this finishes with a pleasing astringency that makes your mouth water for more — it's quickly become a classic for good reason.

Schönramer Surtaler

ABV	3.4%
COUNTRY OF ORIGIN	Germany
GREAT WITH	Grilled cod
ALSO TRY	Hönöbryggeriet Lager 5%, Sweden

This is categorised as a *'Schankbier'*, which is an antiquated tax bracket for lower alcohol lagers in Germany, but, just because it no longer applies legally, doesn't mean it's not a great style to look out for when you are travelling around arguably the lager capital of the world...

Now in its eighth generation of family ownership, having been established in 1780 by farmer Franz Jacob Köllerer, who acquired the estate of the private brewery Schönram, it holds dear its Bavarian roots and ensures that the historic DNA runs through all of its brews.

The beer itself is light, refreshing perfection, walking a tightrope of balance between soft malt character and just a little hint of spice from the hops. A simple beer that harks back to simpler times, well, they probably weren't but with all the chaos in the world, it's nice to think that.

Crooked Stave Von Pilsner

ABV	5%
COUNTRY OF ORIGIN	USA
GREAT WITH	Mushroom pizza
ALSO TRY	Lost and Grounded Keller Pils 4.8%, UK

When you say the name 'Crooked Stave' most people will immediately launch into raptures about founder Chad Yakobson's wild fermented beers, and rightly so, but this is the beer that you are more likely to see him and the brewers crushing at the end of a tough shift.

Based in one of my favourite places in the world, Denver, Colorado, Chad's laidback manner yet deep scientific knowledge of brewing makes him one of my favourite 'beer nerds' to chat to at any given time.

Von Pilsner is an unfiltered Keller (cellar) beer that has the delicious white bread middle that marks out a great German-style Pils, but still has that bright, fresh, clean and absolutely smashable quality about it, which is what makes it a great first drink (or two) whilst you're deciding how complicated you'd like to get with the rest of his magnificent brews.

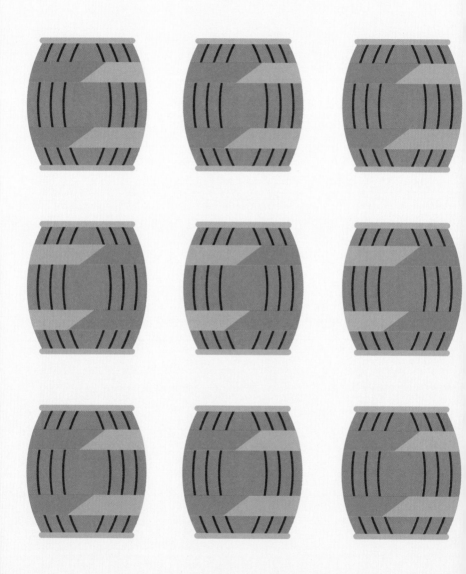

A stave is one of the pieces of wood that is used to make a wooden barrel and sometimes you get a crooked one that you need to replace, which is kind of the ethos of the brewery - a bit wonky! Interestingly, if you look closely at a wooden barrel, you'll notice that not all the staves are the same width. This is where the skill of the cooper, a master barrel maker, comes into play, shaping them to all fit perfectly.

Bavik
Super
Pils

ABV	5.2%
COUNTRY OF ORIGIN	Belgium
GREAT WITH	Fries
ALSO TRY	Fourpure Pils
	4.7%, UK

I have a tremendous soft spot for this beer. When I've been drinking crazy, sour or big alcohol Belgian beers for a few days it comes as a pleasant change, just for its clean, crisp refreshment (especially if I'm somewhere where Brasserie de la Senne Taras Boulba isn't available and look out for its new Zinne lager).

Made at the De Brabandere Brewery, founded in 1894 and now run by the fifth generation of the same family, it has come a long way from a small operation in a shed that had to struggle through two world wars, to being now a truly beautiful, as well as tasty, operation.

The colour of the Super Pils is a striking light gold that has you smacking your lips in anticipation as it pours, with a wispy lemon nose. It is packed with flavour as it is unpasteurised, and has the kind of brisk carbonation that feels like your tongue is being scrubbed by a thousand little bubbly brushes, with a crisp, well-balanced, bitter finish. But, beware, it doesn't seem as strong as it is... take my word for it!

Napar-
bier
Napar
Pils

ABV	4.9%
COUNTRY OF ORIGIN	Spain
GREAT WITH	Manchego
ALSO TRY	Firestone Walker Pivo Pils
	5.3%, USA

Naparbier started up in 2009 when craft beer was all but anathema in Spain, but has grown in stature, not only on its domestic stage, but on the international one too.

The brewery started with its Pils and a Dunkel but quickly grew to love making a wide variety of styles, including a spiced pumpkin ale, and having a strong barrel-aged beer programme.

But back to the Pils: simple, easy drinking with a hint of under-ripe peach and that characteristic herbal character, it is very slightly more acidic than is traditional, but is none the worse for it as it adds an extra layer of refreshment to the beer.

A little bit of advice about drinking draught beer in Spain when it's hot: order a *'caña'* instead of going for larger glasses. This civilised little pour is far superior as it ensures your beer stays cold right to the very end and it has a pleasing aesthetic with tapas or *pintxos* as well: eat small food, drink small beer, repeat – it's not a bad way to socialise!

NOT SO PURE

OK, so this is a tricky one, because on the one hand, I don't want to upset the Germans who, after all, basically gave us lager, but I also want you to understand marks of quality when you see them and, to be honest, the fabled German beer purity law, the *Reinheitsgebot*, isn't guaranteed to be one of them.

Just as a brewery calling itself 'craft' doesn't mean that it's actually either independent or making good beer (although that, of course, in itself, is subjective), the Reinheitsgebot doesn't guarantee that a beer will be free of additives or be any good. So, why do I say that? Well, let me give you a little history behind it first.

Firstly, let's bust one of the most pervasive myths about it: it was not, by any stretch of the imagination, the first law to protect food and drink production.

There are references to food protection laws and edicts in ancient Greek, Chinese, Hindu and Roman writings and, if you think about it, we are probably all aware of food safety 'laws' handed down in various religious texts – the Old Testament being a clear example.

And, when it comes to booze, we've always been pretty keen to make sure that our supply is alright. A notable reference being in Cato the Elder's *De Agricultura*, where he hands down some wisdom on spotting watered-down wine.

Secondly, it's worth noting that no one in the world brews to the original Reinheitsgebot of 1516 because it didn't include any mention of yeast, stating clearly that, 'The only ingredients used for the brewing of beer must be Barley, Hops and Water.'

I say this because anyone claiming to brew to the original law is probably someone's beers you want to avoid if you're looking to get a bit of a buzz on. That's because it's missing the all important yeast, which they just didn't know about as a distinct ingredient (what with a lack of microscopes and cell counts available). And the idea that additional ingredients over and above those core three weren't allowed is also false. As early as the mid-1500s, the law was evolving to allow bay leaf and coriander too, although that would wax and wane over the centuries and eventually be abolished.

And it was almost certainly a lot to do with religious conservatism wanting to forbid the production of beers with ingredients known for their use in 'pagan' rituals.

It's recorded that one of the things that was to be stamped out was the use of fly agaric mushrooms in the brewing process. Now, I don't know about you, but I was always told 'not to eat the red ones' (particularly after reading *Alice in Wonderland* for the first time) because, even though there are very few recorded human deaths from eating these mushrooms, they are pretty toxic.

However, par-boiling breaks down the toxicity of these mushrooms and releases their psychoactive properties (don't try this at home, kids). The use of these mushrooms is widely documented in societies from the Bronze Age, and has been extensively studied in countries all over the world from Siberia to Mexico, but as we progressed as a society, the use of psychoactive substances became more and more frowned upon.

Another important element of the whole equation is that, in essence, the Reinheitsgebot is more of a bread law than a beer law, as it was actually designed to protect the use of grains for food, rather than the purity of beer; thus preventing grains like rye and wheat being used in beer and saved instead for bread.

But, that's enough of history, let me bring you up to date on what the Reinheitsgebot means today.

It's worth noting that whilst the Reinheitsgebot applied to the common folk, it did not apply to the nobility, who continued to brew with wheat. However, they lost interest in doing so in the mid-1800s and only the tenacity of George Schneider, who believed the style to be incredibly important, meant that the rights moved to a 'commoner'. He brewed his first beer in 1872 and the rest, as they say, is history.

Essentially, it's a set of outdated handcuffs for brewing creativity and does absolutely nothing to protect the consumer, and never really has.

It is not a guaranteed mark of quality, as there is nothing in the law that talks about, for example, a lager having to actually lager and mature in the brewery; nor is there a jot about spoilage or how there have to be strict controls on the quality of a beer; it's certainly not advertised that clearing or stabilising agents and artificial sweeteners are allowed and, as long as it's not being sold in Germany, you can do whatever you like with the word.

The Reinheitsgebot was also adopted in Greece, under its first king Otto, who was originally a Bavarian prince and reigned for just 30 years, from 1832–1862, until he was deposed. Colonising German brewers in the Qingdao province of China also voluntarily brewed under it, which is still true today in the production of Tsingtao.

Chapter Two

Brown

Lager that's not light yellow to dark gold? What is this, witchcraft? Well, it's a proud and long tradition of different regional variants and other styles of beer brewed for special occasions like Oktoberfest, and which has been adopted by brewers all over the world.

The transformation in flavour and colour when you alter the malts, even a tiny bit, can make an astonishing change and this is where the light lager training wheels come off! If you don't know what I'm talking about, then well done for skipping to the bit you actually care about — life is short, and there are beers to drink — but it's on page 8 in case you are interested.

VIENNA

Anton Dreher was the inventor of Vienna lager and it, in turn, gave birth to the quintessential märzen brewed by Spaten brewer, Gabriel Sedlmayr (these two had a history of industrial brewing espionage, a story told on page 66).

The beer is built around a base of Vienna malt, which is a pleasing stepping stone into the world of darker lagers, as it doesn't have any roasted characteristic and is ultimately a very drinkable beer that doesn't tend to reach the heady alcohol heights of the märzens. Interestingly, as its popularity waned in Austria and wider Europe, it actually gained popularity in Mexico, where brands like Dos Equis Amber and Bohemia still thrive. Although they have strayed somewhat from their roots, they still have more than a passing nod to their forebears.

TRADITIONAL BOCK BIER

Strong, sweet and very low in hop character, traditional Bock is almost like a sweet, dark bread in a bottle.

MÄRZEN

This isn't just lagering, this is serious lagering! This beer style was traditionally kept from spring until autumn when a law was instituted that prohibited brewing in the summer months (pre-refrigeration, this would have been based around ensuring quality).

Interestingly, it took the place of Dunkel as the official Oktoberfest style of beer and was, in turn, replaced with festbier. It is, however, often the style you'll see at US and some UK Oktoberfests as the beer style of choice — sentimental fools that we are.

DOPPELBOCK

Drunken monks again! Goodness, they did like their booze, huh? Well, this one was definitely created at a monastery, by the Paulaner friars; supposedly, this was their sustenance during lent.

'Doppel' means 'double' and whilst it can be dark gold in colour, most err towards the brown and ruby coloured and taste like a malt loaf with a few shavings of chocolate over the top.

DUNKEL

A deep, rich, dark brown beer that is simply divine used in hearty meat stews and alongside them, and even better for quaffing in pints on dark winter days. I don't know why but, when the weather gets cold, my thoughts turn to a pint of this Munich style of lager as it is both refreshing and comforting in the same breath — weird but true!

EISBOCK

Since time immemorial people have been trying to figure out how to make booze stronger and, probably by accident, someone discovered if you freeze a beer, the alcohol stays liquid and you can condense it, and so Eisbock was born. There have been a lot of ridiculous ABV 'arms races' over the years to make the strongest one, which were mostly undrinkable and just a display of macho nonsense in my opinion, but a good Eisbock is a thing of joy (and I know this book is about lager, but I will say that my favourite is actually a Weizen-Bock, or Wheat Bock, from Aventinus).

Paulaner
Salvator

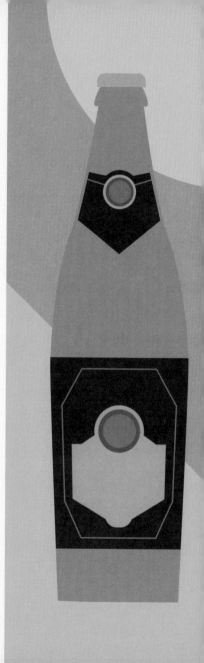

ABV	7.9%
COUNTRY OF ORIGIN	Germany
GREAT WITH	*Schweinebraten*
	(Beer-roast pork)
ALSO TRY	Arboga X-tra Strong
	10.2%, Sweden

If there's one thing you can't ignore when you are writing a book like this, it's the immense brewing history that the German state of Bavaria brings to the table. This beer is like slamming down an ace, moving to checkmate and scoring the winning penalty in football all rolled into one.

The Paulaner Brewery is one of the six breweries allowed to produce beers under the Oktoberfest name in Munich for that most famous of beer festivals, but this is something different altogether.

Paulaner Salvator is, quite simply, a beer that does not muck about. The brewery claims it is the 'father' of all Doppelbock beers.

Whether that is historically accurate or not may be up for some debate, but it's certainly not a youngster, having been brewed for nearly 400 years and having spawned numerous homages, which almost always end in 'ator'. You have been warned!

The beer itself is an absolute riot of boozy cherry, orange liqueur, toffee, raisins and a hint of an almost sandalwood characteristic on the nose. When it hits the palate, the warming alcoholic hit spreads all those flavours out across your tongue, along with a hint of *dulce de leche* and sweet apple, before sliding down your throat to give your tummy a thorough hug.

Narcose Amber Lager

ABV	4.7%
COUNTRY OF ORIGIN	Brazil
GREAT WITH	BBQ picanha steak
ALSO TRY	West Berkshire Vienna Lager 4.8%, UK

Tucked away in Capão da Canoa – a town an hour and a half outside Porto Alegre in Brazil – this is one of the most picturesque breweries you could imagine. It has a view of the mountains and a lake, is mere minutes from the seashore and has a taproom veranda from which you can survey all three. It seriously makes you want to run away and stay there.

The Brazilian beer scene is one that is flourishing overall. With a huge influence from not only the early German and Portuguese immigrants but also now from beer cultures around the world, it has some of the most earnest and educated beer schools in the world. But I digress...

I have to confess that the Diehl family, which owns the brewery, is effectively my Brazilian família. They welcome me with open arms any time I visit, but it's more than that. The beers that are coming out of the brewery are simply perfect for the weather and also innovative, and are starting to pick up multiple awards.

The Amber Lager is probably my favourite easy-drinker from the line up, with bread, digestive biscuit and the teeniest hint of toffee underneath an enticing floral aroma. It is simply perfect with grilled meat, which is pretty much the staple diet in Brazil!

Brooklyn Lager

ABV	5.2%
COUNTRY OF ORIGIN	USA
GREAT WITH	Roast chicken
ALSO TRY	Sierra Nevada Oktoberfest 6%, USA

Brooklyn Lager was a genuine eye opener the first time I had it. Whilst I'd had darker lagers from Germany and the Czech Republic, there was just something so distinctly different about it that I couldn't help but linger over it for a bit, taking it all in, fortunately I was in a bar in New York by myself at the time, so I was drinking it pretty much fresh from source.

Brooklyn can only be described as a tremendous success story in the 'craft' world, it took on a site in, what was at the time, a deeply deprived neighbourhood in New York and put a lot of investment into the area, and has, in recent years, been extremely vocally supportive of the LGBTQ+ community.

It has also been extremely successful on a business level, having bought up some minority shares in other US craft brewers, like Funkwerks in Fort Collins, CO, and one of my personal favourites, 21st Amendment in San Francisco, CA, as well as with one with a rather dubious history in the shape of London Fields in the UK capital.

Now 24.5% owned by Kirin, and in partnership with Carlsberg to produce its beers in Europe, you can expect to see more of its flagship beer, with its rich brioche and marmalade edge and biting nettle hop bitterness.

Gabriel Sedlmyer II of the Spaten Brewery and Anton Dreher, of Dreher Brewery Austria, were responsible for some hilarious brewing industrial espionage in the 1820s and 30s, resulting in the eventual introduction by Dreher of Vienna-style lager. The pair travelled to the UK to learn of new techniques and would regularly abuse the trust of their hosts by pinching wort and yeast samples, via a specially commissioned, valved metal tube (some stories alleging it was hidden in a walking stick). Sedlmyer even recorded in his diary that 'It always surprises me that we can get away with these thefts without being beaten up.'

Cerveja Musa Mick

ABV	4.5%
COUNTRY OF ORIGIN	Portugal
GREAT WITH	Salt cod fritters
ALSO TRY	San Miguel Selecta 6.2%, Spain

Portugal's independent beer scene has seen a sudden explosion in recent years and this brewery is one that's really caught my eye. Born from a road trip where founders Bruno and Nuno (and yes, it's partly because I love the alliteration between their names that I want to tell the story!) fell in love with great beer and began to plan their new venture.

The problem was that they had a missing link. Fortunately it turned out OK because they found Nick Rosich, a brewer who was, for some reason, willing to trade the -20°C (-4°F) Pittsburgh winters for Lisbon's distinctly sunnier climes. He pops back every now and then (one assumes when the thermostat drops) to check that everything is in order at the brewery and the rest, as they say, is history.

This Vienna Lager is an exceptionally bright, clean version of the style, with a tiny bit less malt character than traditional versions. However, it doesn't suffer for it as the amped up floral, herbal hop character more than makes up for the fresher, cleaner body, and it is more suited to the climate as a result.

Texels
Bock

ABV	7%
COUNTRY OF ORIGIN	Netherlands
GREAT WITH	*Appelflappen* (Apple turnovers)
ALSO TRY	Birradamare 'Na Biretta Rossa 6.3%, Italy

There is a certain charm to anywhere that can lay claim to being the site of the only ever naval defeat by people on horseback, and the island of Texel is it. This curious event happened in 1795 when the French army was occupying Holland and received intelligence that the Dutch navy was trapped in ice around this Frisian island. One hundred and twenty-eight men rode up to demand its surrender, which the Dutch navy promptly did without a single shot being fired.

In fact, as a result of its location, the island has had somewhat of a military history – it has also been involved in the American Revolution and WWI to name but two. However, it is a more peaceful story that I wish to tell here.

Brouwerij Texels is a genuinely lovely business, whic has passionate brand ambassadors and even more passionately produced beers, and uses mostly local ingredients. Its flagship brand 'Skuumkoppe' is having a brewery built solely for its production; it has proven that popular.

My favourite, however, is the Bock, a multi award-winning, strong, aromatic lager that will warm the very cockles of your soul. Almost oloroso sherry-like on the nose, it is a deep amber that's also full of garnet highlights. Raisins and prunes dominate the nose with dried apricot and orange peel, and it has a delightfully brisk carbonation. All in all, it is a bit of a boozy delight.

Morada Cia Etílica Double Vienna

ABV	7.6%
COUNTRY OF ORIGIN	Brazil
GREAT WITH	Asado lamb
ALSO TRY	Bronckhorster IJsselbock 7%, Netherlands

The wonderful Fernanda Lazzari and Andre 'Junqa' Junqueira are two of the sweetest folks on the Brazilian beer scene and this is another Brazilian brewery that is like family.

Based in what could easily be considered 'craft beer HQ' in Curitiba, Brazil, they cuckoo brew at several different sites. As well as producing this astonishing Double Vienna, which is created in collaboration with Stillwater Artisanal from the US, they also produce other notable beers. These include the Hop Arabica, which is one of the best coffee beers I've ever tasted… and being terribly British and a tea drinker, I don't even like coffee that much.

Anyway, I digress. There is a huge German influence on the culture and, by extension, the brewing scene in Brazil, although not for the rather unpleasant reason most people think. German immigrants were coming to Brazil from the early 1800s and the first beer brand that was established in Brazil was Bohemia, which still exists to this day. Brazil also holds the world's third-largest Oktoberfest in the delightful city of Blumenau (somewhere that also has a German village, which is a little disconcerting at first as it's a slice of Bavaria in 32°C [90°F] Brazilian heat with an average 80% humidity).

But back to the beer — it does exactly what it says on the bottle: it gives you all of the dry, biscuity caramel drinkability of a Vienna Lager, but with a very deceptive level of alcohol. Approach with joyous caution, as opposed to abandon, or it could end messily!

Chapter Three

Black(ish)

OK, no, seriously, I'm not winding you up here; there really are very dark lagers out there. They are more like a porter or stout in appearance, but still encompass the wonderful, refreshing lager characteristic. They are a palate-twisting, roller-coaster ride of joy.

From the long tradition of negra lagers in Mexico to Germany's stygian offerings, and the Czech-style toffeed styles, these dark horses will amaze you with their complex notes and immense quaffability.

CZECH DARK LAGER

If you are ever in Prague, pay a pilgrimage to U Fleků. Whilst its claim to be the oldest brewpub in Europe may not be entirely ratifiable, it is certainly a site of great interest to beer lovers – and the Czech dark lager on sale is sublime. It's not quite black, more a very deep brown, but has just a hint of roasty smokiness that seems to fit the brooding environment very well. A more commercially available example is Budvar Dark.

SCHWARZBIER

Black as night but still remarkably refreshing, it's one of those beers that I love giving to people who say 'they only drink Guinness' because it seriously messes with their heads (hey, I never said I was a nice person!). Originating from central and eastern Germany, it's only in, historically speaking, more modern times that it became a true lager as it would have originally been warm fermented, most likely with an ale yeast.

BALTIC PORTER

A beer that was originally made for export in the 18th and 19th centuries, this really messes with people's heads when you tell them it's a lager. It is a perfect example of my earlier assertion that lager is more of a process than a style.

Baltic tastes for exported British beer were well documented. Whilst it was a dicey and potentially ruinous undertaking, it could yield financial gains that were worth the gamble, and so breweries like Allsopp and, in turn, Bass gave inspiration for Russian Imperial Stouts.

Köstritzer
Schwarzbier

ABV	4.8%
COUNTRY OF ORIGIN	Germany
GREAT WITH	Rib-eye steak
ALSO TRY	Devils Backbone
	Schwartz Bier
	5.1%, USA

With mentions of its dark beer dating back as far as 1543, the brewery is a true survivor. As a result of its history, it is one of the oldest breweries in Germany, and also one of the longest recorded producers of black beer in the country's history.

As the country's favourite, it has been graced by everyone, including politicians like Angela Merkel and Otto von Bismarck (both of whom are noted diplomats, so perhaps it's down to being mellowed by this tremendous beer, but that's maybe a bit of a reach!).

What is particularly of note, however, is that it is Germany's favourite black beer and is exported to over 50 countries. This definitely marks it out as something quite special in a lager market that prizes cold and clear over nearly everything else.

Full of coffee and toasted notes, with a hint of tobacco and raisins, it's surprisingly light on the palate, making it great to cut through a fattier cut of steak like a rib-eye. In fact, I've been known to brine steak in it before I whack it in a screaming-hot cast iron pan for that extra deep, smoky, roasty touch.

Baeren Schwarz

ABV	5.5%
COUNTRY OF ORIGIN	Japan
GREAT WITH	Tonkotsu ramen
ALSO TRY	Mahou Negra 5.5%, Spain

Gracing the Japanese beer scene for nearly two decades, Baeren has been a mainstay of supporting the growth of 'craft' in Japan – and there's a lot to be said about its philosophy of supporting its communities.

After the awful earthquakes and tsunami in 2011, the brewery decided to brew two beers to support the disaster relief funds. (It should be noted that it was not alone, breweries like Hitachino Nest opened natural water supplies to locals without safe municipal drinking water.)

Very rooted in the German brewing traditions, to the extent that the company not only founded it with a German-trained *Braumeister*, it also bought a one hundred-year-old German brewhouse – lock, stock and barrel – and transported it to Japan. Its black beer has been a core member of its range since pretty much the beginning. The beer ticks all the boxes as a faithful recreation of that dark, coffeed, almost smoky German style and is a surprisingly good foil for the deep, rich porky broth of a tonkotsu ramen.

Bock Damm

ABV	5.9%
COUNTRY OF ORIGIN	Spain
GREAT WITH	*Arroz negro* (Black rice)
ALSO TRY	Mönchshof Schwarzbier 4.9%, Germany

A dark beer in Spain? The land of sun, sea, sand and siesta? Yes, I know it sounds a bit mad but it's incredibly popular and makes a nice change from the normal, fairly interchangeable light lagers.

Another beer that owes its roots to Germany, this is a fairly faithful recreation of the first ever dark beer. (It was created in Einbeck, Germany, in the 14th century and is considered the benchmark for the style.)

Made with a mixture of different malts – heavily roasted black malt, and aromatic and flavoursome caramel malt. The backbone of the whole beer is, as is almost always the case, the pale malt that provides the fermentable sugars.

The combination of the three, along with the busy lager yeast, gives you somewhat the impression of a boozy cold brew. If you get lucky, you might even find it in an outlet that serves it in the traditional stoneware jug – there's something quite ridiculously pleasing about drinking from them!

Xingu
Black
Beer

ABV	4.6%
COUNTRY OF ORIGIN	Brazil
GREAT WITH	*Feijoada*
	(Black bean and meat stew)
ALSO TRY	Moonlight Black to Reality
	5%, USA

Brazil is a hive of creativity in the beer world. It has even come up with its very own beer style called Catarina Sour, but that's for another time (although if you see one, do try it, it's very tasty, but be prepared for some mouth-puckering!).

Xingu can easily be considered the foremother of this busy new brewing culture. The project started in 1986 when five women from Vermont founded Amazon, Inc. after one of the founders, Anne Latchis, married the (now late) Alan Eames, a beer historian and anthropologist. He told her a story about how many Amazonian people considered black beer to be of great spiritual importance in their social and religious rituals. There is also a rich history of native female brewers who fermented grains and roots into black beer, using herbs and bark to bitter the brew.

After taking their honeymoon to make a successful expedition to discover the history of this beer style, the pair teamed up with Brazilian Cesario Mello Franco, who identified a willing brewer to finalise the recipe for a black beer that melded the tradition with more modern techniques. It was designed to honour the idea of the brew rather than directly recreate it and it has won accolades the world over as a result.

The beer brand has now been sold back to the Brazilian people, but is still a source of great pride to Anne and her colleagues. It is a clean, fruity, cold brew-like beer, with a passing similarity to German Schwarzbiers (see page 78), but with a more accessible drinkability.

Kulmbacher Brauerei Eisbock

ABV	9.2%
COUNTRY OF ORIGIN	Germany
GREAT WITH	Rind-washed cheese
ALSO TRY	Samichlaus Schwarzes 14%, Austria

Humans have been trying to get wasted in numerous different ways since Adam was a lad and (apologies to the students that think they've discovered it every new university intake) freezing alcoholic beverages and ridding them of some of the water is just one way that has been used for centuries.

The legend goes that Kulmbacher was the first ever brewery to accidentally leave its Doppelbock (see page 59) out in the yard during freezing temperatures. As water has a warmer freezing point than alcohol, the water comes out of the alcohol in ice crystals. This leaves behind the alcohol and, in effect, concentrates the booze content.

This process, if done well, leaves a worryingly drinkable result behind. It has lashings of liquorice, plums, intense dark caramel and some figgy notes, and a soothing warmth at the end; in fact it almost brings to mind a Christmas pudding in a glass.

Monteith's Black

ABV 5.2%
COUNTRY OF ORIGIN New Zealand
GREAT WITH Smoked fish
ALSO TRY Budvar Dark
4.7%, Czech Republic

If you've ever been to New Zealand's South Island you'll know why so many Scots decided to make it their home. Earthquakes aside, it does feel a lot like the lusher areas of the Scottish Highlands, so it's no real surprise that a brewery with a name that literally means 'hill pasture above the river Teith' gained traction in that area of the country.

The history of the brewery is so twisty turny that if you are curious to know more, then I suggest you hustle on over to their website because I simply don't have enough space here. To give a brief overview, it can trace some of its roots back to 1868 and it is so loved in NZ that when its current owners, DB Breweries (a subsidiary of Heineken Asia Pacific), tried to close the brewery, it lasted exactly four days before it was reopened due to the local outcry.

Monteith's Black has been a stalwart in the line-up over the years, although it is brewed in smaller batches these days as tastes have changed. However, it is still well loved for its complex roast character, combined with its eminently drinkability, slips down smoother than a weka will pick your pocket.

Asahi
Black

ABV	5%
COUNTRY OF ORIGIN	Japan
GREAT WITH	Sea urchin
ALSO TRY	Small Beer Dark Lager
	1%, UK

Asahi's rise in prominence in the last 30 or so years is really quite something. Introducing the first ever 'super dry' lager onto the Japanese scene and using a high proportion of rice to get a seriously high attenuation (fermentation of sugars) drove its popularity through the roof – the dark version shows a more sophisticated side of the style.

Although it was founded in Osaka in 1889, it wasn't until nearly 100 years later that it introduced its 'super dry' variant. This caught the attention of lager drinkers up and down the country so much that it changed its business fortunes dramatically, seeing it overtake Kirin in both volume and value sales.

You shouldn't expect anything too whizz-bang with this beer, but that's OK because its simplicity is a lot of its joy. Less explosive in roast and toast on the palate than its German inspiration, it leaves a little lingering smoke and tobacco in the mouth. And it really does live up to its super dry moniker, making it perfect for hot, humid Japanese nights.

Whilst Japan has Asahi as its super brand, its nearby neighbour, China, has the largest beer brand in the world that you've probably never heard of... Snow. Snow sells nearly double the volume of Budweiser globally, despite selling almost exclusively to its domestic market. I'll be honest though, it's not what you'd call an inspiring beer. It calls to mind an obvious misquoted joke of 'don't drink yellow Snow' but that's just a bit rude and you should always join the locals in a glass or two.

Chapter Four

Hop Stars

You may well have noticed there are a wealth of ales being brewed nowadays that buck the norms, challenge the status quo and are downright weird in places. Well, the same holds true for lager too.

When I say 'hop stars', I mean beers that are brewed in the traditional fashion and then have an extra layer of aromatic or bittering hops added to them. This fundamentally changes the overall impression of the beer. They mess with your head by smelling something like an IPA and yet have all the thirst-quenching aspects of a lager. They always strike me as a little rollercoaster ride for your senses.

Moon
Dog
Beer
Can

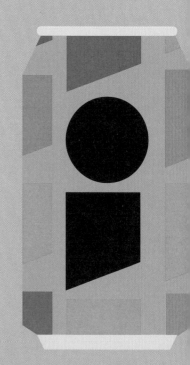

ABV	4.2%
COUNTRY OF ORIGIN	Australia
GREAT WITH	A hot sweaty gig
ALSO TRY	Croucher New Zealand Pilsner 5%, New Zealand

There are times when a beer is so very perfect for the situation you're in that you don't even bother looking at the bar, and this is my abiding memory of trying Moon Dog for the first time.

I was in Australia and we had just finished judging duties so it was time to let our hair down a bit and go dancing. In the hot bar we were in, busting our moves on the dance floor (God, I hope there's no video evidence), can after can of this beer was passed along the line so we could carry on enjoying ourselves with a refreshing beverage in hand, but without letting our inner nerd get in the way.

It just works because even though there is a negligible malt profile, it is packed full of citrus hops. It is designed to be a great version of those somewhat dubious 'tropical' lagers that you need to stick lime in to make palatable. (Sorry, I do try not to be a beer snob, but I'm afraid that's my line in the sand!)

Hopefully, fingers crossed, you'll have just read the first 'snobby' sentence in this book about lager, but there is a good reason for that. I am very sensitive to something called 'light strike', which is prevalent in the average tropical lager, and that's because they are nearly always packaged in clear glass. Clear and green glass offer no and little protection to a beer. Therefore the hop aroma compounds quickly degrade into unpleasant sulphur compounds. I find it quite repulsive but, studies have shown, that it doesn't even register for around a third of the average population. It's also why they suggest you put a slice of citrus in the top of the bottle and glug it from that. I'm not judging you if you do, I'm just saying try it in a glass without the fruit and see if you are sensitive to it!

Coedo Kyara

ABV	5.5%
COUNTRY OF ORIGIN	Japan
GREAT WITH	Garlic prawns
ALSO TRY	Lacons Steam Lager 4.6%, UK

The Coedo Brewery has a fascinating history. It was founded on the principles of local sourcing and organic farming. However, when the owners realised they weren't able to find anywhere to malt the local barley, they looked to a different crop – sweet potatoes – and a new Japanese beer style was born.

However, Kyara is brewed in a more traditional fashion and the name denotes the Japanese word for a deep golden brown colour tinged with red.

Using the gloriously vinous and tropical Nelson Sauvin hop, the beer itself is also complex in the body. It uses six different malts to great effect – each one building to provide a light orangey, rye bread undertone that never dominates or feels cloying. It's a beer that's won multiple awards and, honestly, once you try it, you'll understand why.

Brouwerij De Prael Dortmunder

ABV	6.4%
COUNTRY OF ORIGIN	Netherlands
GREAT WITH	*Bitterballen* (Dutch meat croquettes)
ALSO TRY	Great Lakes Dortmunder Gold 5.8%, USA

De Prael is one of my 'must visits' every time I go to Amsterdam. Co-owner Fer Kok is one of the few people I know in the industry who is louder and madder than I am, so it's always comforting to be around him. Plus, there's also a lot about the physical place and the ethos that makes me respect it a lot too.

Fer worked in psychiatry for years, specialising in people with social and learning problems, and one of his first moves when opening his brewpub was to actively employ people the rest of society would normally leave behind.

But, lofty aims aside, the beer also speaks for itself and a personal favourite is the Dortmunder, which can most easily be explained as a higher-ABV Pilsner but, as with everything de Prael does, it has its own twist. The slightly dank aroma that pours from the glass as you drink it marks it out as having a far higher hopping rate than you'd normally expect from such a style. Beware though, it's dangerously easy to drink and disguises its alcohol content very well... and as the brewpub is on the edge of the red light district, who knows where you might end up!

Birrificio
Italiano
Tipopils

ABV	5.2%
COUNTRY OF ORIGIN	Italy
GREAT WITH	Parma ham
ALSO TRY	Ninkasi Pilsner Cold Fermented Lager 4.7%, USA

If you say 'Tipopils' to any beer aficionado, you will most likely elicit a little sigh of happy memories of sipping on this lager perfection.

It's a big thing to say that a beer is perfect, but this one really is as close as one can get to easy-drinking perfection without being dumbed down. Owner Agostino Arioli is also a perfect drinking partner: wryly funny, humble but incredibly passionate about his beers, and with a sudden smile that can light up a room.

Agostino's background is in science, which is not unusual for brewers or owners, and it's that sense of precision and technical excellence that makes his beers, and his reputation, so very impeccable. Actually, I'll be really honest, he's known as one of the most punctilious nerds in the business, who records every variable going, which reflects in the excellence of his beer.

The beer itself is unfiltered and unpasteurised and can sometimes seem a little hazy, but is none the worse for it. It has a soft peachy aroma that overlays the bread dough aroma from the malt and is as elegant as Milan Fashion Week.

Camden
Town
Brewery
Week
Nite

ABV	3%
COUNTRY OF ORIGIN	UK
GREAT WITH	The sofa
ALSO TRY	Cotswold Brew Co. Haus Lager 4%, UK

Camden Town Brewery pretty much made its name making a lager very cleverly called 'Hells', which is somewhere between a Pilsner and a Helles-style, but it's this one that is easier to reach for as a balm for a busy day.

Former owner, Jaspar Cuppaidge, built the brewery up in London until it caught the eye of the world's biggest beer company: AB-InBev. It snapped up the beer in 2015 and then helped build the already-in-progress site in Enfield, North London. It's always easy to say that 'the beer has got worse' when breweries sell to bigger names, but that accusation cannot be levelled at Camden, as it goes from strength to strength.

Week Nite could easily fool the nose into thinking it's an American-style pale ale, but the glorious zippiness it brings on the palate screams lager and, at just 3%, you can treat yourself to more than one and still have a clear head in the morning.

Week Nite reflects an interesting trend in the UK and Europe, which is that people are looking more and more at lower and no alcohol options. It's partly lifestyle and health related, partly down to the sheer pace and responsibilities that people have, but also due to the fact that younger generations are tending to reject alcohol altogether.

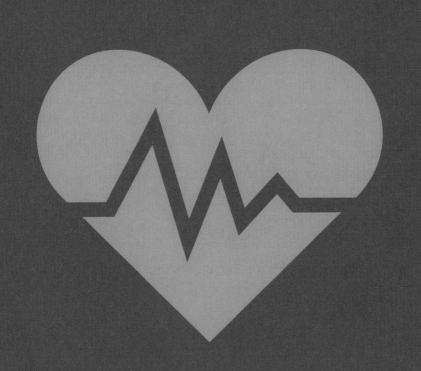

Adnams Jack Brand Dry Hopped Lager

ABV	4.2%
COUNTRY OF ORIGIN	UK
GREAT WITH	A pint of prawns
ALSO TRY	Not For Sale Ale
	Craft Lager
	4.7%, Sweden

Better known for being a traditional ale brewery, Adnams could possibly vie for having the prettiest site for a brewery in the world. Situated in the scenic coastal town of Southwold, it has a long heritage of being family-owned and community-engaged.

It also has a high regard for the environment, being one of the first (if not the first) breweries to actively look for lighter glass bottles and reduce its carbon footprint with its eco-friendly distribution centre. Its head brewer, Fergus Fitzgerald, is also widely regarded as one of the best blokes in beer.

The Dry Hopped Lager makes delicious use of the gloriously peachy/pine Australian hop Galaxy, which brings with it a mouthwatering astringency that makes you want to dive back in for more.

Adnams really does live and breathe its community and sustainability motto – from local beach cleans to grants through its Community Trust – it even has its own beekeeper called Steve!

The company has reduced its carbon emissions by 48% in the last 12 years, saves 1 million litres of water a year through its green roof schemes on its brewery and distribution centre, sends zero waste to landfill, and that's not all. If only more breweries were as socially responsible as Adnams is!

New Belgium Shift Pale Lager

ABV	5%
COUNTRY OF ORIGIN	USA
GREAT WITH	Chicken wings
ALSO TRY	Stone Brewing Tropic of Thunder 5.8%, USA

You can't beat a beer that's been designed to keep thirsty brewers happy at the end of a long shift, and this absolutely ticks that box perfectly.

If you ever get the chance to visit New Belgium in Fort Collins, it is an absolute delight – a beer playground, if you like. Fort Collins, just outside Denver, is somewhere I could happily live, although my liver might disagree as there are amazing breweries in the area. Another big plus for the company is that it is employee-owned*, which makes it a kind of co-operative. This means there's a very high standard of work/life balance.

Shift is packed full of aromatic New Zealand Nelson Sauvin hops, giving it that lovely Sauvignon Blanc aroma, with layers of spicy floral from other varieties, and just enough malt flavour to make it lip-smackingly satisfying.

*At the time of writing this, New Belgium was under offer to Japanese brewer Kirin, and awaiting an employee vote to decide the sale.

Williams Brothers Caesar Augustus

ABV	4.1%
COUNTRY OF ORIGIN	Scotland
GREAT WITH	Lemon meringue
ALSO TRY	Devils Backbone
	Southern Passion
	4.2%, USA

I simply cannot write this section without including the first-ever highly hopped lager I ever encountered. Williams Brothers have been breaking ground in the UK craft beer scene since I can remember.

One of the new wave of family brewers, with the second generation of Williams at the helm. The brewery was founded on a series of wonderful circumstances around the gift of a heather ale recipe. It has now grown, flourished and nurtured brewing talent across the industry for over 30 years.

Caesar Augustus is a vibrant beer that's like lemon meringue in a glass. In fact, I've frequently paired it with lemon curd meringue, much to people's confusion and joy, as it is simply the last word in delicate delight.

Mondo
All Caps

ABV	4.5%
COUNTRY OF ORIGIN	UK
GREAT WITH	Fish tacos
ALSO TRY	Kees Citra Pils
	4.5%, Netherlands

You have to love a story that has a familial memory behind it AND tastes good too. That's definitely the case with Mondo ALL CAPS.

Founded by Todd Matteson and Thomas Palmer, the latter hails from what is arguably the home of US industrial light lager: St Louis. He also has brewing heritage as his father, uncle and grandfather all worked at the brewery.

However, young Thomas may not have always been the best behaved lad, and whilst on a 'forced absence' from school he was required to accompany his father to work for a day, which is where he discovered the joys of the unfiltered, undiluted 6% tank version of America's favourite beer. That flavour was to stick in his mind for years to come.

Fast forward to six months into production at his, and business partner Todd Matteson's, own brewery, in the shape of Mondo, in West London. Inspired by that flavour memory, and spurred on an impending visit from a Japanese friend who only drank lagers, Thomas came up with ALL CAPS. It sits somewhere in between the super-dry Japanese style and an all-American classic.

The resulting lager has an updated American classic, with the slightly sweet, maize-like edge you'd expect but with more heft from the classic European bittering hops and a breezy orange pith aroma and finish.

Chapter Five

Hybrids

Remember when I said back at the beginning that lager is really more a process than it is an actual style? Well, these beers fit perfectly into that description.

Initially made as if they were going to be an ale, using the common ale yeast strain *Sacchoramyces cervisiae* that ferments at a warmer temperature than lager yeasts, these beers then undergo the lagering process. It creates something that looks and tastes almost identical to the traditional idea of a lager but, if you pay a little bit more attention, they have something different about them.

Früh
Kölsch

ABV	4.8%
COUNTRY OF ORIGIN	Germany
GREAT WITH	People watching
ALSO TRY	Howling Hops
	Das Köolsch
	4.6%, UK

If you'd like to see an ignominious scuffle between beer nerds, just ask them which is their favourite Kölsch – Gaffel or Früh – and there's a distinct possibility it'll come to blows.

OK, so I'm exaggerating a bit, but for such a delicate beer style it does seriously raise some very strong feelings in people. I'm afraid, I come down on the side of Früh.

Maybe this is because it was the first Kölsch I was aware of drinking. My late friend Glenn Payne got me one and, halfway through it, he asked me what I thought. He never asked idle questions when it came to beer, so I stopped and assessed it and realised I was drinking something a little more special than 'just a lager'. (Forgive me, I was younger and less educated then!)

Früh is a delicate delight, particularly when drunk fresh at source in Cologne. It's a beer I always get a delicate hint of lychee from, which I assume comes from its warmer fermentation. However, it's that cold lagering period that really gives it that crisp, lightly bready, totally palate-pleasing finish, which makes you reach for tiny glass after tiny glass of it.

Orbit
Nico

ABV	4.8%
COUNTRY OF ORIGIN	UK
GREAT WITH	Salted peanuts
ALSO TRY	Fuller's Frontier 4.5%, UK

When I found out a UK brewery was going to be making a Kölsch I was unbearably excited and, boy, oh boy, does this deliver.

Initially I was a bit sceptical as it had a far more aromatic nose than I was expecting, and then I realised that this is what an unfiltered version of the Cologne-style would smell like. Sadly, because it strips out a lot of the aroma and flavour compounds, you lose a lot when you subject a beer to this process; most especially in a simple, delicate beer style like this.

However, within minutes I realised I'd got to the bottom of my glass without even noticing. If you can say that about any beer you drink, or brew, then I think you can be happy in your decisions!

With a light, overripe pear note and a hint of white pepper on the nose, along with a gorgeous effervescence and ephemeral, fruity, slightly bitter finish, I can't think of many beers I'd rather reach for at the end of a hot, cramped tube (subway) journey.

Uerige Altbier Classic

ABV	4.7%
COUNTRY OF ORIGIN	Germany
GREAT WITH	Pretzel and cheese dip
ALSO TRY	Duckstein Altbier 3.7%, Australia

I am a huge fan of Altbier; in fact, I love it so much that I keep pestering a local-to-me brewery to bring it back to their list. Sadly, I appear to be a fairly lonely lover of this style in the UK's capital. Luckily though, I can take solace in this truly excellent version.

It's extremely rare that you'll find a bottle-conditioned beer in Germany. This is a process where you make the beer in the usual way, but then you give it a secondary ferment in the bottle with either the residual yeast in the beer or by adding a little dose to the bottle and some fresh yeast. This does a number of things: firstly, it very efficiently scavenges any excess oxygen in the bottle, which is good for keeping the beer fresh, and, secondly, it also creates a smoother carbonation with some extra flavour as a bonus.

This classic German variety is probably the most robust and full-flavoured of any of the traditional Altbiers still being produced in Germany. It has a lightly gingery note, huge soft, fresh pretzel middle and a peppery spice at the end that makes you cluck your tongue in delight.

Anchor Steam Beer

ABV	4.9%
COUNTRY OF ORIGIN	USA
GREAT WITH	Mission-style burrito
ALSO TRY	Hammerton Islington Steam Lager 4.7%, UK

There is so much to say about Anchor Brewing in San Francisco – not least about its owner from 1965–2010, Fritz Maytag, and legacy as a forefather of craft beer in America.

You may recognise the Maytag name, as the family were inventors of the modern-day washing machine. A 25-year-old Fritz, seeing that the brewery's fortunes were on the wane, decided that he would stake much of his inherited wealth on reviving its fortunes. Flying in the face of the 60s stock market 'bear' state, he gave away more and more of his stock to save the brewery, much to his family's dismay. Eventually, however, his investment in positioning the brand as a premium product paid off, and it went on to become an American icon.

There are many legends and myths around why it's called 'steam beer', which is also now known as California Common, but what can't be argued are its roots in the German Altbier style. The rich, malt body is instantly recognisable as such, but there's a little extra tang from the Northern Brewer hops grown in the US, which add an almost over-blown orange peel punch with a hint of nettle.

Les Trois Mousquetaires Sticke Alt

ABV	6%
COUNTRY OF ORIGIN	Canada
GREAT WITH	Classic reuben
	(or better still,
	Montreal smoked meat)
ALSO TRY	Põhjala Öö
	10.5%, Estonia

As my mum hails from Montreal, it is always nice to be able to put a beer in from her home province. This one is a cracker.

Les Trois Mousquetaires (I don't think that needs much translation!) is over 15 years old and still fighting fit, and was one of the early founders of Canada's vibrant microbrewery culture. Like so many of its fellow French descendants, it is fiercely proud of its Quebec heritage and sources its malt from the province. Unlike many of its counterparts, it looks more to traditional European styles than to its hopped-up neighbours in the South.

With a bit more body than a traditional Alt beer, this is a deep ruby, with all the rich bready and slightly hazelnut flavours and aromas you'd expect. However, it has a bit more heft from the traditional European hops, which provide a strong peppery and almost cut-grass overtone, lifting the body slightly and making it ideal to pair with gamey or smoked meats.

Baltika No.6 Porter

ABV	7%
COUNTRY OF ORIGIN	Russia
GREAT WITH	Smoked salmon
ALSO TRY	Põhjala Öö
	10.5%, Estonia

I bet you weren't expecting something called porter to turn up in this book, but it's a testament to how beer styles can change so fundamentally when they move across borders.

Once again, this is a style that has much myth and legend about it. To put it simply, porters were exported from UK breweries to the Baltic states a lot in the 19th and early 20th centuries. When successive wars dried up that supply, local breweries took up the mantle. With all the tradition being more based around lagered beers, this was the type of yeast used and that's how this style came about. This may upset the purist beer historians because of its simplification, but it's the easiest way I can explain it in such a short space of time.

If you want to know more, I strongly recommend reading the works of Ron Pattinson and Martyn Cornell.

But, back to the Baltika... I have literally lost count of the amount of awards this beer has won in the Baltic porter category because it absolutely nails the style. In fact, it's used as one of the classic style examples in competition guidelines, it's that classic.

Coffee, dark roast and a lashing of liquorice with an overtone of astringent redcurrant, it's a complex and fascinating beer that you have a tendency to look at faintly confused when you take your first ever sip, before diving back in for more.

Chapter Six

Oddballs

The great thing about the world of craft/artisan beer is that it allows a huge degree of artistic freedom, much of which would have the good burghers of Bavaria biting through their brewing record books.

Here you will find lagers that have been aged for many more months than is usual and historic beer styles that are being re-imagined and have moved sufficiently away from their roots. These beers that have fruit, spices or other things added to them, and offer the adventurous drinker the option to explore a little more widely.

Wild Beer Co. Sleeping Limes

ABV	4.6%
COUNTRY OF ORIGIN	UK
GREAT WITH	Fish tacos
ALSO TRY	Lindeboom Citroen Radler 2%, Netherlands

The Wild Beer Co. has been an utter revelation for the UK brewery scene – it was pretty much the first brewery in the UK to run a full wild ferment and barrel-ageing programme and continues to innovate as it grows older.

The two founders, Andrew Cooper and Brett Ellis, met whilst working at Dark Star Brewery, now part of Asahi. Together they fell in love with Belgian mixed-fermentation beers and began to dream, and dream big, about what it was they could do with that passion. They found a place on a farm down in picturesque Somerset and started to plot and plan how they could make beers in that style but, intelligently, realised that these take time and they needed to make money in between.

So, they launched a series of 'drink fresh' beers that quickly won accolades and this is one of the more recent ones to join that range. Born from (the aptly-named) Brett's, love for Mexican food, this is technically a lager, but it almost masquerades as a gose, with its big sour hit of lime and pinch of sea salt at the end. I could write more tasting notes but, honestly, that's what it simply is, and it is delicious for it.

The reason I say that Brett is aptly named is because, in the beer world, the wild yeast *Brettanomyces* – which features so heavily in so many of Wild Beer Co.'s beers – is frequently shortened to 'Brett'.

Flying Monkeys
12 Minutes To Destiny

ABV	4.1%
COUNTRY OF ORIGIN	Canada
GREAT WITH	Tuna nigiri
ALSO TRY	Surly Brewing Rosé 5.2%, USA

When an idea is right, it's right. The name of this beer tells you everything you need to know about how long it took to nail this delightfully fresh and fragrant lager.

Founded by Peter Chiodo, the brewery loves to hire passionate and talented home brewers and its motto is 'brew fearlessly', which is to be applauded in an age when big beer marketing budgets could possibly take you out in a heartbeat.

Based in Ontario, the taproom knows how to welcome people in, with a vast array of pinball machines and classic arcade games, as well as great food on offer. So you can settle in and enjoy the stay.

This particular beer is made with hibiscus flowers, rose hips, fresh raspberries and orange peel; as you can imagine, it is a complete riot of fruity, floral flavours and aromas, with a good bop of citrus bitterness at the end... in all honesty, it's simply summer in a glass.

Stiegl Radler Grapefruit

ABV	2%
COUNTRY OF ORIGIN	Austria
GREAT WITH	A long bike ride
ALSO TRY	Rothaus Radler Zäpfle 2.4%, Germany

Just think about it: you've decided that you are going to squeeze yourself into some Lycra and head off for a spin; maybe you think you can take on a mountain stage in Austria? If you're not gasping for a beer at the very thought, then I'm afraid we might not be friends.

But, if you are, then a Radler is your go-to buddy here. Most of the traditional ones are based on lagers. Notable versions include Germany's Schöfferhofer and 'craft' versions like the UK's Marble Sunshine Radler based on a simple wheat beer, but all of them are like nectar from the gods after a serious bout of exercise.

Originally designed to refresh cyclists without high alcohol levels, this is one of my particular favourites. In fact, Stiegl is just a good all round brewery and the first in Austria to practise an organic approach. (Stiegl is a brewery with a long and fascinating history, see page 117 for its links with Mozart and more!)

Pithy, bright, grapefruit flavours, middling carbonation and without anything cloying on the back of the throat, it slips down in big gulps that are nearly always followed by a satisfied 'ahhhh' at the end.

Beer and music have long been bedfellows. From 'Hymn to Ninkasi' (which also happens to be the oldest known recipe for beer in the world) to Beck's* 'Beercan', you see a lot of breweries and bands teaming up to create collaboration beers these days.

*to be clear, I mean the singer here! Not the beer brand.

Hogs Back Montezuma's Chocolate Lager

ABV	4.5%
COUNTRY OF ORIGIN	UK
GREAT WITH	*Hong shao rou*
	(braised pork belly)
ALSO TRY	Sam Adams Chocolate Bock
	5.8%, USA

Chocolate lager. Choc-o-late-larrr-gerrr... yep, that's what I said, sounds mad, doesn't it? This particular beer is what can only be described as a proper mind melter – a blonde lager that tastes of chocolate. Your brain doesn't want to believe it, even as your palate is experiencing it.

What makes it even more surprising is that it comes from what is perceived as a seriously traditional brewery in the depths of leafy Surrey, a county just outside London. However, when brewery owner, Rupert Thompson, met with the founders of Montezuma's chocolate, they hatched a plan to make a beer that would twist people's brains, and they definitely succeeded in that mission.

Taking a pure chocolate essence, they made multiple blends with the brewery's lager before finally settling on the one they liked best. The finishing result was a lightly chocolate flavoured, mildly sweet lager with the merest hint of bittering balance.

Against The Grain Bloody Show

ABV	5.5%
COUNTRY OF ORIGIN	USA
GREAT WITH	Fried chicken Kentucky style
ALSO TRY	Hitachino Nest Yuzu Lager 5.6%, Japan

You know when you meet people and you can see EXACTLY why they've called their business something like 'Against the Grain'? Well, these chaps are certainly living their brand.

Founded by Jerry Gnagy, Sam Cruz, Adam Watson and Andrew Ott, this brewery is a collection of the mad, bad and dangerous to know, with a penchant for tongue-in-cheek naming conventions that extends far beyond the brewery's name.

A true Southern success story, the brewery has gone from a small operation with an attached smokehouse in 2011 to adding a production brewery just a few blocks away that sees the company's beers in 43 states and 25 countries in just a few short years.

The Bloody Show is clearly designed for those hot, sultry Kentucky days, when the air barely moves and you can almost feel an attack of the vapours coming on.

Originally a collaboration with Danish brewery Mikkeller, it is packed full of orange peel and blood orange purée and lots of fresh complementary hops like Mosaic and Huell Melon.

But, drinker beware, it may taste like the poshest shandy you've ever drunk, but it does pack a pithy punch.

Biera
Corsa
Pietra

ABV	6%
COUNTRY OF ORIGIN	Corsica
GREAT WITH	Cheese beignets
ALSO TRY	The Nuts Cheslic Lager 4.1%, New Zealand (GF)

You have to love people who have a passion for a product and, because they can't drink any local beer, decide to change that dynamic entirely.

So when Armelle Sialelli and her husband Dominique were sitting one evening in 1992, lamenting that they couldn't drink any Corsican beer, they decided to set out and change that.

The island has a long-standing reputation for natural resources – one of which is chestnuts. They employed a professional brewer and decided to brew with the addition of chestnut flour, which undoubtedly gives the beer an added sweet but not cloying piquancy. However, it still finishes refreshingly clean and also makes you a little hungry for some reason!

Another thing I love about this brewery is the strong female representation they have amongst their staff. On such a tiny island, they have managed to get a better gender ratio than lots of breweries in big cities. I admire that.

Chapter Seven

Gluten-Free and Alcohol-Free

Whether you are choosing to avoid alcohol or gluten, or need to do so for your health, you'll be delighted to know that you can now get tasty versions of both.

The issue of gluten-free can, however, be a sticky one. In some countries you can only call something gluten-free if it has been brewed with grains that don't contain any gluten. In others, like the UK, you can use an enzyme to break down the gluten and, provided it's below a certain threshold, it is considered fine. However, if you have a severe gluten allergy it is worth checking which type you are drinking or seek medical advice.

Alcohol-free has similarly complex connotations, but, as a general rule of thumb, anything 0.5% alcohol or below is safely considered alcohol-free and that's how I'll be proceeding here.

Big Drop Lager
(GF/AF)

ABV	0.5%
COUNTRY OF ORIGIN	UK
GREAT WITH	Halloumi salad
ALSO TRY	Pistonhead Flat Tire Alcohol Free 0.5%, Sweden

When founder Rob Fink realised that his legal practice was leading him to drink more than he'd like, he cast around for genuinely enjoyable non-alcoholic beers and came up pretty blank. So he decided to do something about it. He hired a brewer who knew what he was doing in Johnny Clayton and the rest, as they say, is history.

Using a 'lazy' yeast that produces very little alcohol, the company has now gone from strength to strength. It produces what are widely recognised as some of the best low-/no-alcohol beers in the UK, and is set to conquer the world if Rob has his way.

The lager is one of the few in the range that doesn't contain lactose (milk sugars), so is also vegan-friendly as well as being gluten-free. Plus, it certainly hits the nail on the head of that refreshing hit you want from a lager at the end of a busy day or a sweaty workout.

Light amber and with a slight fresh hay and subtle caramel nose, it finishes with a pleasant pepperiness that really lights the whole affair up. It's a welcome change from the bland and boring low-alcohol lagers of the past.

Lucky Saint

ABV	0.5%
COUNTRY OF ORIGIN	Germany
GREAT WITH	Steamed white fish
ALSO TRY	Free Damm 0.0%, Spain

It's interesting that a lot of the modern alcohol-free beers have been created by people fed up with not being able to drink a decent commercially available version and this, like Big Drop, was created for exactly that reason. Founder Luke Boase worked with four different breweries before finally finding one in Germany that could create the unfiltered, quality lager he was looking for.

As opposed to a lot of alcohol-free beers that boil the booze off, which tends to give sickly sweet results, this goes through a much more gentle removal of the alcohol after it has been brewed.

When you add the careful alcohol removal process to the fact that it has been matured for a proper lagering period of over a month, you end up with a beer that has a lot of that bready flavour and rounded mouthfeel you'd expect from a German lager, with a pop of herbal hops at the end.

Stiegl Freibier

(AF)

ABV	0.5%
COUNTRY OF ORIGIN	Austria
GREAT WITH	*Weinerschnitzel* (Viennese Schnitzel)
ALSO TRY	Sagres 0.5%, Portugal

There really aren't a lot of breweries that are still in existence and can claim that they've been visited by Wolfgang Amadeus Mozart, but Stiegl can. Being the sad case that I am, I've actually sat with one of this beer's full-blooded cousins and listened to a Mozart flute concerto and I can attest that it's a very pleasant experience.

My long-lapsed love for that particular woodwind instrument aside, this really is the real deal when it comes to excellent alcohol-free beer. It doesn't really surprise me because there is little Stiegl puts a foot wrong on.

As with most of their other beers, the ingredients are all sourced from Austria. Unfiltered to ensure maximum flavour, it has an unusually spicy tangerine pop on the nose and palate from the local Saphir hops.

Sobah
Lemon
Aspen
Pilsner
(AF)

ABV	0.5%
COUNTRY OF ORIGIN	Australia
GREAT WITH	Shellfish
ALSO TRY	Kingfisher Radler Ginger & Lime 0%, India

There's lots to celebrate about the Sobah brand. Owned and led by Aboriginals, it is the first alcohol-free dedicated brewery in Australia and believes in treading lightly and acting ethically.

As with all beers, it's designed to live in a social space, but the purpose of this enterprise extends far beyond that. The brewery also highlights some of the social issues that affect the indigenous population and breaks down a lot of the associated stereotypes; instead championing the positive contributions the Aboriginal and Torres Strait Islanders make to Australian society.

Rather charmingly calling itself 'bush tucker beer', the vegan-friendly Pilsner uses a native fruit – lemon aspen – which produces a bright, fresh, almost pink grapefruit flavour and aroma. (There's also a super-tasty finger lime Mexican-style lager in the range.) It is so unbelievably perfect for the hot weather you get in Australia that all I could think of was golden sands and surfing when I tried it.

Brewing with herbs and other botanicals came long before hops, and these beers would have been better known as 'gruit ales'. They would have been spontaneously fermented, meaning they would probably have been quite funky and probably quite sour, but a source of booze and food in one nonetheless.

Westerham Helles Belles (GF)

ABV	4%
COUNTRY OF ORIGIN	UK
GREAT WITH	Fresh pretzels
ALSO TRY	Green's Gluten Free Glorious Pilsner 4.5%, UK

Westerham Brewery has been quietly making gluten-free beer for quite some time, but not really shouting about it. That's typical of the people who own it. They just get on with making really good beer that, for the most part, happens to be gluten-free, so I thought I'd shout for them.

Having worked in the city for a long time, owner Robert Wicks decided to jack it all in and become part of the town's proud brewing tradition. He even references some classic brews from the old Eagle Brewery that once stood very close to where his brand new brewhouse (with a rather lovely taproom) stands now.

Helles Belles, as the name suggests, is a Helles-style lager with all the easy-drinking character you'd expect. Brioche flavours abound in the excellently structured but light body, and it is redolent with herbal, spicy Hallertau Tradition hops, which you only need one sniff of to be immediately transported to Munich.

Brewing with things other than barley requires the use of external, but still natural, enzymes to break down the starches into fermentable sugars. This technology has been pioneered by companies like Guinness for use in beers in countries where growing barley is difficult, like Nigeria, so the beer can be brewed locally.

Celia Dark

(GF)

ABV	5.7%
COUNTRY OF ORIGIN	Czech Republic
GREAT WITH	Pork knuckle
ALSO TRY	Voll-Damm
	7.2%, Spain

A dark, gluten-free lager is a rare beast indeed. In fact, if there is another commercially available one in the world, I haven't been able to find it (which is not to say there isn't, of course, I am knowledgeable but not all-seeing!).

Brewed in the beautiful historic Czech town of Žatec at the now Carlsberg-owned site, the brewery dates back to the 1700s and the lagering caves are still dug into the castle walls. (It is also home to some exceptionally good porter, but that's another story for another book!)

Deepest ruby brown, the beer has strong depths of coffee and chocolate, but with a fresh berry note and light body that allows it to be both complex and refreshing at the same time.

Wicklow Wolf Moonlight

(AF)

ABV	0.5%
COUNTRY OF ORIGIN	Ireland
GREAT WITH	A day's fly fishing
ALSO TRY	Guinness Pure Brew 0.5%, Ireland

Wicklow Wolf's beers were some of the first I tried from Ireland that I was impressed with and they have gone from strength to strength ever since.

Again another brewery that was influenced by the American beer scene, it was founded by two friends, Quincey Fennelly and Simon Lynch, who say it was an 'inevitability' that they would end up in the brewing business together.

With staff now comfortably in double figures, the brewery even has its own 10-acre hop farm – a rarity indeed in Ireland. It's flourishing under Lynch's watchful eye and no doubt benefits from his 20 years in the horticultural industry.

The beer itself is almost indistinguishable from a full-blooded American-style pale ale, redolent with grapefruit Citra hops but with the added white grape note that comes from the European Hallertau Blanc hops too – a delightful sipping beer when idling away some hours on a bank, dangling a rod in the water. (And I speak from experience of dangling rods in the water, it's the catching of the damn fish that all too frequently eludes me... still, at least I always have a decent beer or two!)

O'Brien Lager
(GF)

ABV	3.5%
COUNTRY OF ORIGIN	Australia
GREAT WITH	A beach sunset
ALSO TRY	Omission Lager
	4.6%, USA

Sometimes you just want to sit back and enjoy a seriously easy-drinking lager at the end of the day whilst watching the sun go down, and this O'Brien one ticks exactly that box.

I won't tell you it's anything that's going to rock your world, because sometimes you don't want that. You just want to drink a well-made lager that is going to ease your mind and soul and that isn't going to interfere with watching the world go by and this, my friends, is exactly that.

A simple, light, clean body with a hint of thyme and lemon, it will hit the spot at the end of a long week at work whilst keeping your head clear at just 3.5%.

Whilst Australia is now synonymous with lager drinking, the very first beer officially recorded was in fact a beer made from corn and cape gooseberry leaves by one John Boston in 1796. Sadly, he then engaged in some commercial trading activities that led him to land on one of the Tongan islands, where he and his seven shipmates were killed by locals.

About
the Author

Award-winning writer, Melissa Cole, is widely acknowledged as one of the UK's leading beer and food experts. Renowned for her insightful and engaging writing style, sense of humour and ability to translate complicated beer jargon into something everyone can understand. From judging beer competitions from Amsterdam to Rio and Denver to Dublin – to brewing with some of the world's most respected breweries like Fuller's, Odell and Goose Island – she is also sought after by restaurants like the world-famous St. John to help construct beer lists. Regularly commissioned to write for national media titles, and appear on radio and TV, she is also a popular face at some of the country's largest food and drink festivals. This is her fourth book.

Acknowledgements

Firstly, as ever, Ben; how you continue to put up with my globe-trotting, disorganisation and general selfishness I have no idea... but you do and for that I thank you and love you very much.

Kate, thank you for your design advice and input. I am more proud of you than you can ever know and I love you fiercely, and the same goes for you, Josh.

Family Eaton, as ever, I thank you all for your support and love; I know I can turn to any of you at any time.

To my industry family and loved ones, you are too numerous to mention all by name but I want to give special love to Mike Hill and Richard Dinwoodie. I say it every time but you were the first people to really give me belief and support in what I wanted to achieve; you mean the world to me.

I'd also like to add special thanks to some folks for being my eyes on the ground in different countries and pointing me in the right directions: Sandra Ganzenmüller, Maik van Heerd, Dan Ihrelius, Glenn Harrison, Todd Nicholson, Martyn Railton and the Euroboozer team, Felipe Devila; and, as ever, I am indebted to the works of Roger Protz, Ron Pattinson and Martyn Cornell.

And to my long-suffering non-industry friends, who I see all too infrequently, thank you for putting up with my bullshit — you are superstars. And to anyone and everyone who ever comes to any of my events, thank you from the bottom of my glass, seeing happy faces whilst drinking beer is what keeps me doing this.

Hannah Valentine, you've done such a beautiful job breathing such personality and life into the book with your design and illustrations; I adore them, thank you so much.

Last, and by no means least, the team at Hardie Grant. Eila Purvis, thank you for working so closely with me to get this one done — I hope it hasn't been too much of a baptism of fire for you! Kajal Mistry, as ever, your support and friendship means the world. Ruth Tewkesbury, your tireless work to get publicity is nothing short of miraculous and, Emma Marijewycz, thanks for putting up with me at festivals in the past year — you're braver than most! And to the rest of the team that work tirelessly for all the authors, you are simply wonderful — thank you.

Index

Index

Published in 2020 by Hardie Grant Books,
an imprint of Hardie Grant Publishing

Hardie Grant Books (London)
5th & 6th Floors
52–54 Southwark Street
London SE1 1UN

Hardie Grant Books (Melbourne)
Building 1, 658 Church Street
Richmond, Victoria 3121

hardiegrantbooks.com

British Library Cataloguing-in-Publication Data. A
catalogue record for this book is available from the
British Library.

The Little Book of Lager
ISBN: 978-1-78488-330-0

10 9 8 7 6 5 4 3 2 1

Publishing Director: Kate Pollard
Commissioning Editor: Kajal Mistry
Editor: Eila Purvis
Art Direction: Hannah Valentine
Copy-editor: Kay Delves
Proofreader: Sharona Selby
Indexer: Cathy Heath

Colour reproduction by p2d
Printed and bound in China by
Leo Paper Products Ltd.